# Playtime for Zoo Animals

by Caroline Arnold     photographs by Richard Hewett

Carolrhoda Books, Inc./Minneapolis

How do zoo animals play?
The same way you do.

**orangutans**

Elephants hold tails
and follow one another.

**elephants**

A baby lion gets ready to pounce.

**lions**

An ostrich runs fast.

ostrich

**A** monkey balances
on a log.

**monkey**

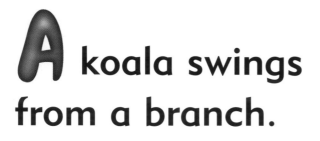 koala swings
from a branch.

koala

A young ibex jumps
at its shadow.

**ibex**

Zebras prance.

**zebras**

17

A parrot tugs on a stick.

**parrot**

 tiger catches a ball.

**tiger**

A baby chimpanzee reaches high.

**chimpanzees**

**Y**oung orangutans climb ropes.

**orangutans**

A baby panda hangs from a jungle gym.

**panda**

Zoo animals play in
many different ways.
How do you like to play?

**sea lion**

# Where can I find...

**hippopotamuses**

Caroline Arnold has written more than one hundred books for children. Many of the books are about animals. Caroline lives with her husband in Los Angeles, California.

Richard Hewett worked for magazines before he discovered children's books. He, too, has created many books about animals. Richard lives with his wife in Los Angeles, California.

Text copyright © 1999 by Caroline Arnold
Photographs copyright © 1999 by Richard R. Hewett
Additional photographs courtesy of: © Caroline Arnold, cover, p. 21

*This book is available in two bindings:*
ISBN 1-57505-287-3 (lib. bdg.)
ISBN 1-57505-391-8 (trade bdg.)

Carolrhoda Books, Inc., c/o The Lerner Publishing Group
241 First Avenue North, Minneapolis, MN 55401 U.S.A.

Website address: www.lernerbooks.com

Library of Congress Cataloging-in-Publication Data

Arnold, Caroline.
    Playtime for zoo animals / by Caroline Arnold ; photographs by Richard Hewett.
       p.   cm.
    Includes index.
    Summary: Photographs and simple text introduce zoo animals at play.
    ISBN 1-57505-287-3 (lib. bdg. : alk. paper)
    1. Zoo animals—Behavior—Juvenile literature. 2. Play behavior in animals—
Juvenile literature. [1. Zoo animals. 2. Animals—Play behavior.] I. Hewett, Richard, ill.
II. Title.
QL77.5.A84   1999
636.088'9—dc21                                                    98-24380

Manufactured in the United States of America
1 2 3 4 5 6 – JR – 04 03 02 01 00 99